OKAPI

By Rachel Rose

Minneapolis, Minnesota

Credits
Cover and title page, © llaurent789/Adobe Stock; 3, © Edwin_Butter/iStock; 4–5, © Jiri Hrebicek/iStock; 7, © ondrejprosicky/Adobe Stock; 8, © Marcel Schauer/Adobe Stock; 9, © Rixipix/iStock; 10–11, © meunierd/Shutterstock; 12–13, © Thorsten Spoerlein/iStock; 14, © Bertrand Godfroid/Adobe Stock; 15, © Ji/Adobe Stock; 17, © Joseph Hendrickson/Shutterstock; 19, © Fotos 593/Adobe Stock, © Sarah.Camille/Adobe Stock; 21, © Gleb_Ivanov/iStock; 22L, © draco77/iStock; 22R, © Therd oval/iStock; 23, © slowmotiongli/iStock.

Bearport Publishing Company Product Development Team
President: Jen Jenson; Director of Product Development: Spencer Brinker; Managing Editor: Allison Juda; Associate Editor: Naomi Reich; Associate Editor: Tiana Tran; Art Director: Colin O'Dea; Designer: Kayla Eggert; Product Development Assistant: Owen Hamlin

STATEMENT ON USAGE OF GENERATIVE ARTIFICIAL INTELLIGENCE
Bearport Publishing remains committed to publishing high-quality nonfiction books. Therefore, we restrict the use of generative AI to ensure accuracy of all text and visual components pertaining to a book's subject. See BearportPublishing.com for details.

Library of Congress Cataloging-in-Publication Data

Names: Rose, Rachel, 1968- author.
Title: Okapi / by Rachel Rose.
Description: Minneapolis, MN : Bearport Publishing Company, [2025] | Series: Library of awesome animals | Includes bibliographical references and index.
Identifiers: LCCN 2023059669 (print) | LCCN 2023059670 (ebook) | ISBN 9798892320221 (library binding) | ISBN 9798892325004 (paperback) | ISBN 9798892321471 (ebook)
Subjects: LCSH: Okapi--Juvenile literature.
Classification: LCC QL737.U56 R67 2025 (print) | LCC QL737.U56 (ebook) | DDC 599.638--dc23/eng/20240124
LC record available at https://lccn.loc.gov/2023059669
LC ebook record available at https://lccn.loc.gov/2023059670

Copyright © 2025 Bearport Publishing Company. All rights reserved. No part of this publication may be reproduced in whole or in part, stored in any retrieval system, or transmitted in any form or by any means, electronic, mechanical, photocopying, recording, or otherwise, without written permission from the publisher. Bearport Publishing is a division of Chrysalis Education Group.

For more information, write to Bearport Publishing, 5357 Penn Avenue South, Minneapolis, MN 55419.

Contents

Awesome Okapis! 4
Creatures of the Rainforest 6
Spot the Difference 8
Terrific Tongues 10
Eat Up 12
Threat from Above 14
In Danger!.......................... 16
A Stand-Up Kid..................... 18
Leaving Home 20

Information Station 22
Glossary 23
Index 24
Read More 24
Learn More Online 24
About the Author 24

AWESOME Okapis!

RUSTLE! A long neck and giraffe-like face appears between the leaves of the forest. But what follows is truly bizarre. The okapi (oh-KAHP-ee) has the striped behind of a zebra. Stretched and striped, okapis are awesome!

OKAPIS ARE ALSO KNOWN AS FOREST GIRAFFES. THEY ARE THE GIRAFFE'S ONLY LIVING RELATIVE.

Creatures of the Rainforest

Wild okapis are found only in the **tropical** Ituri Forest of central Africa. Their odd **adaptations** are a perfect fit for this tree-filled home. Okapis have thick, reddish-brown fur that keeps them dry in the wet forest. The stripes on their legs and behinds help them blend in. The pattern **mimics** the bands of sunlight that shine through the trees.

> OKAPIS USED TO LIVE IN EAST AFRICA, TOO, BUT THEY HAVE BECOME **EXTINCT** THERE.

Spot the Difference

While their bottoms make them look like zebras, the okapis' top halves make them look like smaller versions of their giraffe cousins. Okapis have long necks and the same face shape as giraffes. **Male** okapis have a similar kind of horn as giraffes, too. **Female** okapis have knobby bumps on their heads instead of horns.

MALE OKAPI HORNS ARE OFTEN SHORT, BUT SOME GROW TO BE ABOUT 6 INCHES (15 CM) LONG.

A female okapi

Terrific Tongues

Another thing okapis have in common with giraffes are their large, dark tongues! Their tongues can grow up to 14 in. (36 cm) long. The animals can use their tongues to clean out their eyes and ears. They are one of the few animals in the world that can lick their own ears!

OKAPIS ALSO USE THEIR LONG TONGUES TO SWAT AWAY UNWELCOME FLIES.

Eat Up

The okapi's long tongue comes in handy for stripping leaves off trees, too. **MUNCH!** The animal eats more than 100 kinds of plants, as well as different fruits and mushrooms. Sometimes, it even eats bat poop. The okapi spends most of its time looking for its next meal. An okapi can eat more than 60 pounds (25 kg) of food in a day.

OKAPIS CAN GRASP AND HOLD THINGS WITH THEIR STRONG, FLEXIBLE TONGUES.

Threat from Above

The okapi also has large, upright ears. This helps it hear. If the animal catches a sound, it quickly runs away. But excellent hearing doesn't always work against its main **predator**, the leopard. This big cat can climb trees, spying its **prey** from above. The leopard waits quietly, and then . . . **POUNCE!** It's all over for the okapi.

OKAPIS ARE FAST. THEY CAN RUN ABOUT 35 MILES PER HOUR (55 KPH).

In Danger!

Sadly, humans are an even bigger threat to okapis than any natural predators. People are destroying their rainforest home by cutting down trees for new buildings. As a result, okapis are **endangered**. However, some groups are trying to save the forest where these amazing animals live. They have fought to stop people from cutting down trees in the Ituri Forest.

> Even though it is illegal, some people hunt and kill okapis for their meat and fur.

A Stand-up Kid

Okapis typically live alone. They come together briefly to **mate** and then are back to solo life. About 16 months later, the female gives birth. A mother okapi usually has just one baby at a time. A young okapi is called a calf. The calf can stand on its wobbly legs about 30 minutes after being born.

> OKAPI CALVES DON'T POOP UNTIL THEY'RE ABOUT A MONTH OLD. THIS HELPS STOP PREDATORS FROM SMELLING THEM.

Leaving Home

The mother stays with her calf for the first few months. Her main job is to keep the little one safe from predators. She **communicates** with her calf by making sounds that other animals, including humans, can't hear. About six months later, the young okapi is ready to leave its mother and take care of itself.

SCIENTISTS BELIEVE WILD OKAPIS LIVE FOR ABOUT 20 TO 30 YEARS.

Information Station

OKAPIS ARE AWESOME!
LET'S LEARN EVEN MORE ABOUT THEM.

Kind of animal: Okapis are mammals. Most mammals have fur, give birth to live young, and drink milk from their mothers as babies.

More tropical forest animals: Many animals live in the Ituri Forest, including the Eastern Lowland Gorilla and the Congo Peacock.

Size: Okapis are about 5 feet (1.5 m) tall. That's about the same height as a small car.

OKAPIS AROUND THE WORLD

Where Okapis Live

Glossary

adaptations special skills or parts of the body that help animals survive

communicates shares information with others

endangered being in danger of dying out completely

extinct when a plant or animal has died out completely

female an okapi that can give birth to young

male an okapi that cannot give birth to young

mate to come together to have young

mimics copies something else very closely

predator an animal that hunts and eats other animals

prey an animal that is hunted and eaten by another animal

tropical having to do with warm areas near the middle of Earth

Index

adaptations 6
Africa 6
calf 18, 20
endangered 16
females 8, 18
giraffe 4, 8, 10
humans 16, 20
Ituri Forest 6, 16, 22
males 8
mate 18
predator 14, 16, 18, 20
tongue 10, 12
zebra 4, 8

Read More

Coupé, Jessica. *Okapi (Animals of the Rainforest).* New York: Lightbox Learning Inc., 2022.

Dufresne, Emilie. *Endangered Animals in the Rain Forests (Endangered Animals).* New York: The Rosen Publishing Group, Inc., 2022.

Learn More Online

1. Go to **www.factsurfer.com** or scan the QR code below.
2. Enter "**Okapi**" into the search box.
3. Click on the cover of this book to see a list of websites.

About the Author

Rachel Rose writes books for kids and teaches yoga. Her favorite animal for all time is her dog, Sandy.